Total Life

Football as a Way of Living

Vaibhav Joshi

COPYRIGHT PAGE

Total Life

Football as a Way of Living

ISBN: 978-93-5759-326-7

First Edition, 2026

Published independently by

Vaibhav Joshi

India

For permissions and inquiries:

vaibhavjoshi0027@gmail.com

DEDICATION

For those who learned life
not through certainty,
but through staying.

AUTHOR'S NOTE

This book did not begin as a book.

It began as an accumulation of moments, some clear, many confusing, where football quietly explained things life never said out loud. Not in slogans. Not in answers. Just in patterns.

I never set out to extract lessons from the game. I played, watched, lost, waited, returned, and noticed that the same questions kept appearing, on the pitch and off it.

How do you respond under pressure?
When do you move, and when do you wait?
How much do you hold, and when do you let go?
Who do you become when things do not go your way?

Football does not ask these questions politely. It forces them, repeatedly. Over time, I realized life does the same thing, just with longer consequences and fewer whistles.

This is not a book about football strategy.
And it is not a book about fixing yourself.

It is a book about attention.

About noticing how you show up when things arrive faster than you expected. About understanding that control is often quieter than force. About learning that love, discipline, patience, and resilience do not announce themselves, they reveal themselves over time.

I did not write this to motivate you.
I wrote it because I needed language for experiences I did not want to rush past anymore.

If anything in these pages feels familiar, it is because you have already lived it, perhaps without naming it. This book does not claim authority over your life. It simply offers a way of seeing.

Read it slowly.
Put it down when something lingers.
Come back when the timing feels right.

Like the game, life does not reward urgency nearly as much as it rewards presence.

And if this book does anything at all, I hope it reminds you that you do not need to play louder, harder, or faster to live fully.

You only need to stay in the game long enough to understand it.

TABLE OF CONTENTS

1: Kick-Off: Starting Right

"Every game begins the same way. A whistle. A breath. A decision to move."

The Weight of the First Whistle

There is something unsettling about kick-off.

Not exciting, unsettling.

Before the whistle, everything is hypothetical. Plans feel safe. Intentions sound intelligent. You can imagine yourself playing well without having to prove anything. The moment the whistle blows, imagination loses its protection.

Now it is real.

I have noticed this strange thing about beginnings, they do not feel like hope. They feel like exposure. The field opens up, there is nowhere to hide. Whatever you are today has to show up, even if it is unfinished, unconfident, or unsure.

Football does not give you time to settle into your nerves. The ball moves immediately. Whether you touch it in the first minute or the tenth, you are already part of the match.

Life does the same thing.

We like to believe we will start when we are ready. When we have improved a little more. When we have thought things through properly. But readiness is an illusion we use to stay comfortable. The truth is that beginnings rarely feel clean. They feel rushed, mistimed, premature.

And that is exactly why most people avoid them.

They mistake hesitation for preparation.
They mistake waiting for wisdom.
They mistake fear for intuition.

I have done this more times than I would like to admit.

No one talks enough about how emotionally expensive it is to begin something that matters.

Starting exposes your inexperience.
It reveals how little you actually know.
It puts your self-image at risk.

Before you start, you are protected by potential. After you start, you are judged by reality.

That is a hard transition.

In football, players feel it in the opening minutes. Touches are cautious. Passes are safe. There is a collective nervousness, not because anyone doubts their ability, but because everyone understands the stakes of the first mistake.

Life mirrors that experience.

You start a new phase, a job, a relationship, a personal commitment, and suddenly everything feels louder. Doubts multiply. You replay small missteps in your head. You become hyper-aware of how you are perceived.

It is not weakness.
It is vulnerability.

And vulnerability always feels like risk to a mind that prefers control.

Beginning Honestly

We romanticize good starts. We talk about hitting the ground running and setting the tone early. These phrases sound inspiring, but they quietly create pressure. They suggest that if you do not begin confidently, you have already failed.

Football tells a different story.

Some of the best performances begin awkwardly. A misplaced pass. A heavy touch. A moment of hesitation. Then gradually, rhythm arrives.

Life works like that too.

A messy beginning does not ruin the journey. It introduces it.

Starting right has nothing to do with starting perfectly. It has everything to do with starting honestly. Showing up as you are, not as who you think you should be.

Momentum is often overrated in the beginning.

People love momentum. They chase it. They wait for it. They assume it is the engine of progress.

But momentum is a byproduct, not a requirement.

You get fit by playing.
You gain clarity by moving.
You build belief by surviving imperfect starts.

Beginnings are not meant to feel powerful. They are meant to feel possible.

The bravest players are not the ones who start confidently. They are the ones who start despite uncertainty. They involve themselves in the game even before they feel ready.

That is courage.

Not loud confidence.
Quiet willingness.

Life rewards the same energy.

You do not need certainty to begin. You need consent. You need to agree to participate in your own life, even when the outcome is unclear.

Fear will always appear at kick-off. Muscles tighten. Thoughts speed up. You imagine mistakes before they happen.

Fear is not trying to stop you. It is trying to protect you. The problem is that it confuses uncertainty with danger.

You do not need to eliminate fear. You need to stop letting it decide.

Let it sit in the stands. It does not need to play.

The Quiet Agreement

Starting small is still starting.

Football begins with a single touch from the center circle. Not a sprint. Not a dramatic play. Just a tap that puts the game in motion.

Life begins the same way.

A conversation you have been avoiding.
A quiet commitment you make to yourself.
A decision you do not announce.

You do not owe the world a perfect start.

You do not need to explain why you are beginning now instead of earlier. You do not need to perform confidence to be allowed to begin.

Life does not keep score of how long you waited. It only responds to whether you showed up.

At kick-off, there is an unspoken agreement.

You accept that mistakes will happen.
You accept that rhythm will take time.
You accept that learning comes through participation.

Life asks for the same contract.

When you begin something, you are not committing to success. You are committing to presence. To learning in public. To staying when it would be easier to retreat.

Whenever I hesitate to begin something important, I try to remember this.

No one feels ready at kick-off.
They simply feel present.

Presence is enough.

You do not need to see the entire match. You only need to step into the first few minutes.

The game will teach you the rest.

2: First Touch: First Reaction

"Your first touch defines your next move. Your first reaction shapes your life."

The Power of the First Touch

In football, the first touch is everything.

It dictates your trajectory. It sets the pace. It decides whether you are in control or at the mercy of chaos. A good first touch buys time. A poor one creates pressure instantly.

When you watch the game closely, you begin to notice how much happens in that first contact with the ball. The body adjusts. The angle changes. Space either opens or closes.

A composed first touch looks simple, but it is rarely accidental. It is the result of repetition, awareness, and quiet preparation.

Life works the same way.

Every situation you encounter arrives like a ball at your feet. You do not choose when it comes. You only choose how you receive it.

Your first reaction is your first touch.

And that reaction often determines what happens next.

Controlled Touch, Controlled Direction

A rushed first touch in football usually comes from panic.

You feel pressure before it is fully there. You imagine the tackle before it arrives. You hurry the moment, and in doing so, you create the very chaos you were trying to avoid.

Life mirrors that pattern.

A critical comment feels like an attack.
An unexpected problem feels like a threat.
A difficult conversation feels like something to escape.

So you react quickly, defensively, emotionally, instinctively.

Once you do, the direction is set.

A good first touch is not only technical. It is intentional.

When a player receives the ball under pressure, the real question is not whether they can control it. The question is where they take it next.

Forward.
Sideways.
Backward.

That decision shapes the next few seconds of the match.

In life, the same choice appears constantly.

When something unexpected comes your way, your first response determines whether the moment expands or contracts. Reacting with anger narrows space. Reacting with calm creates it.

Control is not about suppressing emotion. It is about choosing direction.

Instinct and Preparation

Some moments in football stay with us because they reveal what preparation looks like under pressure.

A single touch that shifts the angle.
A controlled reception that opens the field.
A movement that feels effortless because it has been practiced thousands of times.

The player is not improvising. The player is executing something rehearsed.

Life rewards that same quiet preparation.

Your first reaction rarely begins in the moment. It begins long before. It is shaped by your habits, your fears, your values, and your past experiences.

If your default response is impatience, it will appear automatically.
If your default response is composure, it will appear just as naturally.

You do not rise to the moment.
You fall to your level of preparation.

The Psychology of Reaction

Your first reaction happens before logic fully arrives.

It is instinctive. Emotional. Conditioned.

That is why it matters so much.

Do you tense when challenged, or do you listen?
Do you interrupt when uncomfortable, or do you breathe first?
Do you withdraw when uncertain, or do you stay present?

These reactions do not just shape isolated events. They shape patterns.

Small reactions accumulate.

A thoughtful word builds trust.
A rushed response creates distance.

A calm pause invites understanding.
A defensive tone closes conversation.

Life is rarely altered by dramatic decisions alone. It is shaped by repeated first reactions.

Practicing the First Touch

Footballers practice first touches endlessly.

Under pressure.
In motion.
With limited time and space.

Life requires similar rehearsal.

Pause before responding. Even a single breath changes tone.
Observe fully before reacting. Let the moment arrive.
Reflect afterward. Notice what worked and what did not.

You do not need perfect reactions.
You need conscious ones.

A composed first touch does not only control the ball. It builds momentum.

When a player receives the ball calmly, the team settles. Movement becomes more confident. Options appear.

Your reactions influence others in the same way.

Calm spreads.
So does panic.

Momentum is often born in the first few seconds of a moment.

Trusting Your Response

One of the hardest lessons in football is trust.

Trust your training.
Trust your instincts.
Trust that preparation will surface when needed.

First touches look spontaneous because they are supported by repetition.

In life, when your reactions are grounded in principles rather than impulse, they rarely betray you. Even if outcomes are imperfect, integrity remains.

You do not need to react quickly.
You need to react truthfully.

Closing Reflection

Life does not wait for ideal conditions.

Opportunities arrive at speed. Challenges appear unannounced. You cannot always control what comes toward you, but you can influence how you receive it.

Every word.
Every decision.
Every pause.

Each one is a first touch.

Make it deliberate.

Let it shape your direction, not your fear.

3: Playing in Position: Knowing Your Role

"You do not need to be everywhere. You only need to be honest about where you belong."

The Confusion of Wanting to Do Everything

One of the earliest lessons football teaches you is that chaos can look like effort.

When you are young, you chase the ball everywhere. You run harder than everyone else. You feel involved. You feel useful. For a while, that works. Energy hides inefficiency.

But eventually the game becomes faster. Smarter. More demanding.

Running everywhere stops being admirable. It starts becoming a liability.

You arrive late.
You leave space open.
You exhaust yourself.

At some point, someone tells you something simple.

Hold your position.

Life has a similar moment.

There comes a time when trying to be everything to everyone stops working. You feel stretched, mentally, emotionally, physically. You are busy but not effective. Present but not impactful.

And slowly, a question begins to surface.

What is my role, really?

Why Role Feels Like Limitation

We resist the idea of roles because they sound restrictive.

A role feels like a box. A boundary. A ceiling.

We want to believe we are capable of anything at any time. And maybe we are. But capability is not the same as alignment.

In football, a defender can score. A striker can track back. A midfielder can tackle. But when everyone tries to do everything, structure collapses.

Life follows the same pattern.

Just because you can do something does not mean you should. Just because you are adaptable does not mean you should live in constant adaptation.

Living without clarity of role creates quiet resentment. You begin doing things out of obligation rather than intention. You say yes too often. You carry responsibilities that were never meant to be yours.

And because you are capable, people allow it.

That is the danger.

Identity Versus Function

Understanding your role does not mean shrinking your identity.

Your role is not who you are. It is how you contribute.

In football, positions are not about hierarchy. They are about function. A defensive midfielder may never score, yet the game depends on their balance and awareness.

In life, we often attach value to visibility. To recognition. To applause.

So we drift toward roles that look important, even if they drain us.

I have seen people abandon roles they were built for because they were not glamorous. I have seen others cling to positions that exhausted them because stepping back felt like failure.

Knowing your role is not about ambition. It is about honesty.

Where do you contribute naturally?
Where does effort feel purposeful instead of forced?
What drains you faster than it should?

These questions matter more than titles.

The Strength of Staying in Your Lane

There is a certain calm that comes when you stop chasing relevance.

When you understand your role, urgency softens. You stop reacting to everything. You respond only to what belongs to you.

In football, players who understand positioning do not look busy. They look available. They arrive early. They simplify the game for others.

Life feels lighter when it works this way.

You stop overexplaining.
You stop overcompensating.
You stop trying to prove your value constantly.

Instead, you trust that your contribution is enough.

That confidence does not shout. It settles.

Misplaced Effort Is Still Misplaced

Effort is praised without question.

We admire people who do it all. Who sacrifice endlessly. Who stretch themselves thin.

But effort without alignment slowly erodes you.

In football, running without positioning creates gaps and fatigue. In life, it creates burnout and resentment.

You can work incredibly hard and still feel misplaced.

That feeling is not weakness. It is information.

Discomfort does not always mean you are failing. Sometimes it means you are playing out of position.

Learning When Not to Intervene

One of the most difficult lessons in both football and life is restraint.

Not every ball needs to be chased. Not every situation needs your involvement.

Sometimes the most responsible action is stepping back.

This feels counterintuitive. We want to help. We want to fix. We want to be useful.

But usefulness is not constant activity. Sometimes it is quiet stability.

Stepping back is not withdrawal when it is done consciously. It is trust.

Trust in others.
Trust in structure.
Trust that not everything depends on you.

That kind of trust is humbling. It is also freeing.

Roles Evolve

Knowing your role does not mean freezing yourself in one version of who you are.

Footballers change positions over time. Speed fades. Vision sharpens. Responsibilities shift.

Life does the same.

The role that suited you once may not suit you now. Clinging to it out of nostalgia can limit growth.

The key is not loyalty to a title. It is attentiveness to who you are becoming.

What feels natural now that once felt forced?
What feels forced now that once felt natural?

Those answers reveal change.

The Cost of Playing Out of Position

When you consistently play out of position, something begins to fracture.

You feel unseen.
You feel misunderstood.
You feel constantly off balance.

That discomfort is not random.

Life is not asking you to try harder. It may be asking you to stand where you belong.

Belonging is not external validation. It is internal coherence.

When your actions align with your nature, effort feels lighter. Even difficult days feel purposeful.

Closing Reflection

Knowing your role does not shrink your life.

It focuses it.

It gives you permission to stop pretending. To stop chasing validation through exhaustion. To stop confusing movement with meaning.

You do not need to be everywhere on the field.

You need to be honest about where you are meant to stand.

And when you are, the game simplifies.

Not because it becomes easier.

Because it finally makes sense.

4: Passing and Possession: The Art of Connection

"Holding the ball feels safe. Letting it go at the right moment keeps the game alive."

The Illusion of Control

There is a stage most players go through when holding the ball feels like security.

As long as it is at your feet, nothing can go wrong. No one else can misplace it. No one else can make the wrong decision. Control feels concentrated.

For a moment, it feels powerful.

But football does not reward possession that refuses to move.

Hold the ball too long and pressure arrives. Space disappears. Options close. What once felt like control becomes confinement.

Life mirrors this pattern closely.

We hold conversations longer than necessary. We hold responsibilities that exhaust us. We hold emotions that should have been released.

We tell ourselves we are being responsible. Reliable. Strong.

Sometimes we are simply afraid to let go.

Possession Is Not Ownership

In football, possession does not mean ownership. It means stewardship.

You are trusted with the ball for a brief moment. The purpose is not to keep it. The purpose is to circulate it.

The game depends on movement.

Life operates under similar rules.

People are not possessions.
Opportunities are not permanent.
Moments are not meant to be trapped.

You are trusted with things for a season. Relationships. Influence. Roles. The health of those things depends on how you pass them forward.

Connection breaks when possession becomes control.

Why Passing Feels Risky

Passing is an act of trust.

The moment the ball leaves your foot, the outcome is no longer entirely yours. Someone else must receive it well. Someone else must make the next decision.

That uncertainty creates hesitation.

In life, passing looks like delegation. Like honesty. Like asking for help. Like allowing someone else to lead.

It requires vulnerability.

You accept that things may not be done exactly the way you would do them. You accept that mistakes might occur.

But you also accept something else.

Growth requires participation from more than one person.

You cannot build rhythm alone.

Overholding Creates Isolation

A player who never passes eventually isolates themselves.

Teammates stop making runs. Movement becomes static. Frustration grows.

The same happens in life.

When you carry everything yourself, others slowly step back. Not because they do not care. Because you have not made space for them.

Overholding is not strength. It is fear disguised as responsibility.

Letting go at the right moment keeps connection alive.

The Rhythm of Shared Movement

Good teams do not just pass well. They move with understanding.

They learn tendencies. They recognize patterns. They anticipate space before it opens.

This takes time.

Missed passes.
Miscommunication.
Adjustment.

Life relationships work the same way.

Connection is not instant chemistry. It is built rhythm.

You learn when to speak. When to listen. When to step forward. When to create room.

Passing is not about abandoning responsibility. It is about distributing it.

Emotional Possession

Sometimes what we hold is not responsibility, but emotion.

Resentment that was never expressed. Expectations that were never clarified. Words that were never said.

Carrying these things quietly feels like maturity. Often it becomes weight.

In football, a tired player who refuses to release the ball becomes predictable. In life, emotional overholding distorts perception.

You begin reacting from stored tension instead of present reality.

Passing emotionally looks like expression. Boundaries. Forgiveness. Acceptance.

It is choosing movement over stagnation.

Knowing When to Keep It Simple

One of the most underrated skills in football is the simple pass.

Not every moment requires creativity. Not every situation demands brilliance.

Sometimes the most intelligent decision is the obvious one.

Life becomes unnecessarily complicated when we search for dramatic solutions.

Say what you mean.
Do what you promise.
Release what is no longer yours to carry.

Simple passes keep the game moving.

Trusting the Return

Passing is rarely one directional.

When done well, the ball returns. Maybe not immediately. Maybe not from the same angle. But the rhythm continues.

Trust requires believing that releasing control does not mean losing involvement.

You do not disappear when you pass. You reposition.

You stay available.

In life, letting go does not remove you from the equation. It changes your role within it.

Closing Reflection

Life, like football, is designed for movement.

Holding everything feels safe in the short term. In the long term, it creates pressure.

Letting go at the right moment is not weakness. It is wisdom.

You do not lose yourself by passing.

You remain part of the play.

And when connection flows, the game does not just continue.

It comes alive.

5: Vision and Awareness: Seeing Beyond the Ball

"What you see determines how you move. What you fail to see determines what surprises you."

The Danger of Narrow Focus

In football, beginners watch only the ball.

Their eyes follow its movement obsessively. Wherever it goes, they go. It feels logical. The ball is the center of the game.

But as the game becomes faster, something changes.

The best players are not staring at the ball. They are scanning the field. They notice runs forming before they fully develop. They sense pressure before it arrives.

Their awareness extends beyond what is immediately visible.

Life rewards the same kind of vision.

When you focus only on the immediate task, the immediate problem, or the immediate emotion, you miss the larger pattern unfolding around you.

Narrow focus creates reaction.
Wide awareness creates choice.

Seeing the Space, Not Just the Action

Experienced players often speak about space more than about the ball.

Where is it opening?
Where is it closing?
Where will it be in the next second?

The game is rarely about the current position of the ball. It is about where it is going.

In life, awareness functions similarly.

A conversation is rarely about the sentence being spoken. It is about the direction it is moving. A challenge is rarely about the moment of difficulty. It is about what it is shaping in you.

If you respond only to what is obvious, you will always be slightly late.

Awareness gives you time.

The Practice of Scanning

Scanning in football is subtle. A quick glance over the shoulder. A turn of the head before receiving the ball. A small adjustment of position.

These movements look insignificant, yet they prevent panic.

A player who scans knows what options exist before pressure arrives.

In life, scanning means paying attention before crisis forces attention.

You notice tension building in a relationship before it explodes.
You sense fatigue in your body before it becomes illness.
You recognize dissatisfaction before it becomes resentment.

Awareness reduces shock.

It does not eliminate difficulty, but it removes surprise.

The Cost of Blind Spots

Every player has blind spots.

Moments when awareness narrows. When attention slips. When focus becomes self-centered.

That is when mistakes occur.

In life, blind spots are often emotional.

Pride that refuses correction.
Fear that avoids conversation.
Insecurity that distorts perception.

Blind spots are not character flaws. They are areas where awareness has not yet matured.

The problem is not having blind spots. The problem is refusing to acknowledge them.

Growth begins when you admit that what you see is incomplete.

Seeing Teammates Clearly

Vision is not only about space. It is about people.

Great players recognize the strengths of those around them. They pass into a teammate's movement because they understand how that person thinks.

Life connection depends on the same attentiveness.

You cannot relate deeply to someone if you only see your own perspective. Awareness requires stepping outside yourself long enough to notice how others move through the world.

What motivates them?
What worries them?
What do they need that they do not articulate?

Seeing clearly reduces unnecessary conflict.

Often disagreement is not opposition. It is misalignment in awareness.

Patience Within Awareness

Seeing everything does not mean acting immediately.

Sometimes awareness asks for restraint.

In football, recognizing space does not mean rushing into it. Timing matters. Move too early and you are offside. Move too late and the opportunity disappears.

In life, awareness without patience becomes anxiety.

You anticipate problems before they exist. You imagine outcomes that have not arrived. You prepare for battles that never occur.

True awareness includes calm.

You see what is forming, and you wait for the right moment to respond.

Vision as Responsibility

With greater awareness comes responsibility.

If you see something others do not, you cannot pretend ignorance.

In football, a player who recognizes danger must communicate. Silence becomes negligence.

In life, awareness sometimes requires courage.

You notice unhealthy patterns.
You recognize unfair dynamics.
You see your own contribution to conflict.

Awareness is not comfortable. It asks you to respond differently.

But it also offers clarity.

Closing Reflection

The ball will always attract attention.

It is loud. Immediate. Urgent.

But the game is shaped by what happens around it.

Life is the same.

What you focus on expands. What you ignore eventually surprises you.

Widen your awareness.

See beyond the obvious.

When you do, movement becomes intentional instead of reactive.

And the field begins to make sense.

6: Scanning: Reading the Field of Life

"The game is faster than you think. The only way to slow it down is to see it before it arrives."

The Habit of Looking Up

In football, scanning is a habit.

Before the ball reaches you, you look up. You check your shoulders. You notice movement behind you. You observe pressure building. These glances take less than a second, yet they change everything.

A player who does not scan is always surprised.

Surprise creates panic. Panic creates rushed decisions. Rushed decisions create mistakes.

Scanning does not eliminate pressure. It prepares you for it.

Life moves just as quickly.

If you only react when something lands directly in front of you, you will constantly feel behind. The conversation escalates before you realize it. The responsibility multiplies before you anticipate it. The opportunity disappears before you recognize it.

Looking up changes timing.

Reading Before Receiving

The best players do their thinking before the ball arrives.

By the time they receive it, the decision is already forming. They know where the space is. They know who is available. They know what pressure is coming.

The touch becomes simple because the awareness was prepared.

Life rewards this same preparation.

If you reflect only after something goes wrong, you will always be in recovery mode. But if you pause regularly to assess where you stand, you regain influence over direction.

Ask yourself simple questions.

Where is pressure building in my life?
What conversation have I been postponing?
What opportunity is forming quietly?

Reading the field before receiving the moment gives you control.

The Discipline of Attention

Scanning requires discipline.

It is easy to become absorbed in your immediate task. It feels productive. It feels focused.

But hyper-focus without awareness creates vulnerability.

In football, a player who stares at the ball forgets about opponents closing in. In life, someone who is consumed by one goal may overlook relationships weakening around them.

Attention must expand and contract.

Focus when necessary.
Zoom out regularly.
Reassess.

Discipline is not constant intensity. It is balanced awareness.

Anticipation Versus Assumption

Scanning is not prediction. It is anticipation.

Prediction assumes certainty. Anticipation recognizes possibility.

In football, you cannot know exactly what will happen. You can only read cues. Body language. Movement patterns. Space.

In life, the same humility applies.

You cannot control outcomes. You can notice trends.

If someone repeatedly withdraws during conflict, anticipate that reaction. If you consistently feel drained in certain environments, acknowledge that pattern.

Anticipation prepares you without locking you into rigid expectation.

Assumption narrows vision.
Anticipation widens it.

Why We Avoid Looking

Sometimes we do not scan because we do not want to see.

Seeing clearly can be uncomfortable.

You might notice that you are overcommitted. That a relationship is unbalanced. That your energy is depleting faster than it should.

Ignoring signs feels easier in the short term.

But unacknowledged patterns grow stronger.

In football, failing to scan does not stop opponents from pressing. It only ensures that you will feel the pressure too late.

In life, avoidance delays understanding. It does not remove reality.

Courage is often quiet. It looks like looking up when you would rather keep your head down.

Communication Through Awareness

Scanning is not a solitary skill.

Players communicate what they see. A shout. A gesture. A warning.

Awareness shared strengthens the entire team.

In life, awareness is also relational.

If you notice tension, address it gently. If you recognize fatigue, express it honestly. If you see growth in someone else, acknowledge it.

What is seen but unspoken creates distance.

What is seen and shared creates connection.

Slowing the Game Down

People often say the game feels slower to experienced players.

It is not that the game changes speed. It is that awareness increases.

When you see more, you react less.

In life, stress often comes from feeling overwhelmed by sudden demands. When you cultivate regular reflection, journaling, conversation, solitude, you reduce shock.

You are rarely blindsided by what you have already considered.

The world remains fast.
Your response becomes steady.

Closing Reflection

Scanning is a quiet habit.

No applause follows a glance over the shoulder. No headlines celebrate awareness.

But without it, everything feels rushed.

Look up.

Not only when you feel pressure.
Not only when something goes wrong.

Look up regularly.

The field is always changing.

The more you notice, the less you panic.

And the more intentional your movement becomes.

7: Patience and Timing: Waiting for the Right Move

"Not every open space is meant to be entered immediately. Some are meant to be waited for."

The Temptation to Rush

In football, space appears and disappears quickly.

When you see an opening, your instinct is to move instantly. To sprint into it. To take advantage before it closes.

Sometimes that works.

Other times, moving too early ruins the opportunity. You arrive before support. You run into pressure. You drift offside.

Timing matters as much as movement.

Life carries the same tension.

When opportunity appears, you feel urgency. When discomfort arises, you feel the need to resolve it immediately. When silence lingers, you rush to fill it.

We confuse speed with decisiveness.

Patience feels passive, but often it is strategic.

The Difference Between Delay and Discipline

Patience is not avoidance.

Avoidance hides from action. Patience prepares for it.

In football, a player may hold their run for a fraction of a second, not because they are hesitant, but because they are reading the defender's position. That pause creates a better angle.

In life, restraint can serve the same purpose.

Waiting before responding to criticism prevents escalation. Taking time before making a major decision reduces regret. Allowing emotions to settle before speaking creates clarity.

Delay out of fear weakens momentum.

Delay with awareness strengthens it.

Understanding Rhythm

Every match has rhythm.

Some moments demand speed. Others demand composure. Players who succeed learn to sense that rhythm. They know when to accelerate and when to recycle possession.

Life moves in rhythms too.

There are seasons of action.
There are seasons of preparation.
There are seasons of quiet growth.

Frustration often comes from misreading the season you are in.

You push when life is asking for reflection. You wait when life is asking for courage.

Timing is less about the clock and more about alignment.

Trusting the Build-Up

Not every meaningful moment is dramatic.

Many goals in football are built through patient sequences. A simple pass. Another pass. A reset. A switch of play. Then gradually, space opens.

The final touch looks brilliant, but the build-up created it.

In life, we often celebrate outcomes while overlooking preparation.

Success rarely arrives without unnoticed groundwork. Healthy relationships rarely appear without consistent attention. Confidence rarely develops without repeated effort.

Impatience interrupts growth.

Trusting the build-up requires belief that what you are doing now, even if it feels small, matters.

The Fear of Missing Out

Impatience is often driven by fear.

If I do not act now, I will lose my chance.
If I do not respond immediately, I will fall behind.
If I do not decide quickly, I will regret it.

Fear shortens perspective.

In football, chasing every opportunity exhausts you. In life, reacting to every possibility scatters your focus.

Sometimes the opportunity that truly belongs to you does not disappear when you pause.

What fades under patience was never stable to begin with.

The Courage to Wait

Waiting requires confidence.

It means believing that your value does not depend on constant motion. It means trusting that the right moment will not require you to abandon yourself.

In football, holding position while others sprint demands discipline. You may feel invisible. You may feel underutilized.

But when the moment arrives, you are balanced. Ready.

In life, patience often looks quiet.

You decline what does not align.
You pause before committing.
You allow uncertainty without forcing resolution.

That stillness is not weakness.

It is control.

When to Move

Patience is powerful, but it is not permanent.

There comes a moment when hesitation becomes regret. When preparation becomes procrastination.

Timing is the art of sensing that shift.

In football, the difference between perfect timing and missed opportunity is often one step. In life, it can be a single decision.

Patience prepares you.
Courage activates you.

The balance between the two creates progress.

Closing Reflection

Rushing feels productive. Waiting feels uncertain.

But timing is rarely loud. It is subtle. It is attentive.

You do not need to enter every space you see.

You need to recognize which ones belong to you.

Wait when patience strengthens your position.
Move when alignment becomes clear.

The right moment does not shout.

It settles.

And when you feel that steadiness, you will know it is time.

8: Managing the Noise: Handling the Chatter Around You

"The loudest voices are rarely the clearest ones."

The Stadium Is Never Silent

No football match is played in silence.

There are chants. Criticism. Applause. Instructions shouted from the sidelines. Teammates calling for the ball. Opponents trying to distract.

The noise is constant.

At first, it feels overwhelming. You try to process everything. Every shout seems urgent. Every reaction feels personal.

Over time, experienced players learn something essential.

Not all noise deserves attention.

Life is no quieter.

Opinions come from every direction. Advice, whether asked for or not. Expectations layered quietly onto your choices. Judgments that may or may not be accurate.

If you attempt to respond to every voice, you lose clarity.

Noise multiplies when attention feeds it.

External Expectations

One of the hardest forms of noise to manage is expectation.

People project their hopes onto you. They assume you should want what they want. They measure your success against standards that may not align with your values.

In football, a player can have a solid performance and still be criticized for not scoring. A defender can prevent danger all match and still be remembered for one mistake.

External perception is unstable.

If your confidence depends entirely on applause, it will disappear the moment criticism arrives.

Learning to separate performance from perception protects your focus.

Internal Noise

The most persistent noise is often internal.

Self-doubt. Comparison. Fear of inadequacy. The replaying of mistakes long after they are over.

In football, a player who dwells on a missed chance struggles to move forward. The game continues whether they are ready or not.

In life, internal criticism can be louder than any external voice.

You question your decisions. You replay conversations. You imagine judgment where none exists.

Silencing the mind completely is unrealistic.

But managing it is possible.

Filtering What Matters

Experienced players do not ignore all noise. They filter it.

A teammate's call for support is valuable. A coach's instruction is useful. Random criticism from the stands is less relevant.

The key is discernment.

In life, some feedback helps you grow. Some opinions expose blind spots. Some voices remind you of your values.

Others distract.

Ask yourself simple questions.

Is this voice invested in my growth?
Is this criticism constructive?
Is this expectation aligned with who I am becoming?

Not every opinion deserves space in your thinking.

The Discipline of Focus

Focus is not about shutting everything out.

It is about choosing what to let in.

In football, focus means staying aware of your role despite surrounding chaos. You may hear the crowd, but your attention remains on the movement unfolding in front of you.

In life, focus means remembering your direction when noise attempts to redirect you.

When someone doubts you, it does not automatically mean you are wrong. When someone praises you, it does not automatically mean you are right.

Stability comes from internal alignment, not external volume.

Responding Instead of Reacting

Noise often invites reaction.

A comment provokes defensiveness. A comparison triggers insecurity. An expectation creates pressure.

Reacting immediately amplifies noise.

Responding thoughtfully reduces it.

In football, players who argue with referees or react emotionally to the crowd lose concentration. The game punishes distraction quickly.

In life, reacting impulsively can escalate minor tensions into lasting conflict.

Pause.

Not every shout requires an answer. Not every misunderstanding requires correction.

Sometimes the most powerful response is composure.

Finding Your Inner Signal

Amid all the noise, there is usually a quieter signal.

Your values.
Your long-term direction.
Your sense of integrity.

That signal does not shout. It steadies.

When you are clear about what matters to you, noise loses power. It may still be loud, but it is less persuasive.

Clarity reduces confusion.

You cannot control what others say. You can control what you prioritize.

Closing Reflection

The stadium will always be loud.

Life will always include opinions, expectations, and doubt.

Silence is not the goal.

Discernment is.

Listen carefully. Filter wisely. Hold your focus steady.

When you know which voices matter, the noise becomes background.

And the game continues with clarity.

9: Fully Trusting Teammates: Faith in Others

"You cannot build something meaningful alone. You can only build it with trust."

The Fear of Dependence

Trust is one of the hardest things to develop in football.

At some point, you must pass the ball without knowing exactly what will happen next. You must believe that your teammate will receive it well, make the right decision, and continue the movement.

If you hesitate, the rhythm breaks.

Yet many players struggle with this.

They prefer to carry the ball themselves. They believe they can control the outcome more reliably than anyone else. It feels safer to depend on your own ability.

Life reflects this instinct.

Relying on others exposes vulnerability. It means accepting that outcomes are no longer entirely in your hands. It means risking disappointment.

So you carry more than you should. You handle responsibilities alone. You limit collaboration because it feels uncertain.

Independence feels strong.

But isolation slowly weakens you.

The Strength of Shared Responsibility

In football, no team succeeds through individual effort alone.

Even the most talented player depends on movement around them. Space is created by others. Defensive coverage is shared. Victory is collective.

Trust distributes weight.

When teammates rely on one another, effort becomes sustainable. Mistakes are absorbed. Confidence grows.

In life, shared responsibility creates resilience.

You lean on others when you are tired. You offer support when they are struggling. Strength circulates.

Trust does not remove accountability. It multiplies it.

Each person becomes responsible not only for their own role, but for honoring the connection.

Learning to Let Others Contribute

Sometimes trust fails because we do not allow others to contribute.

We correct too quickly. We intervene too soon. We redo tasks in our own way.

In football, a player who never trusts teammates with difficult passes limits their growth. Teammates become hesitant. Creativity shrinks.

In life, refusing help sends a message.

It suggests that others are not capable. It suggests that your standards matter more than shared growth.

Letting others contribute may involve mistakes. It may require patience.

But growth demands participation.

Repairing Broken Trust

Trust is not always seamless.

There are missed passes. Miscommunication. Decisions that do not align.

In football, trust is rebuilt through continued effort. Through honest conversation. Through persistence.

In life, disappointment can tempt you to withdraw completely.

If someone fails you, it feels easier to close off. To reduce dependence. To protect yourself from further hurt.

Protection has its place.

But complete withdrawal isolates you from possibility.

Trust does not require blindness. It requires discernment.

You learn from experience. You adjust expectations. You communicate boundaries.

Then, carefully, you try again.

Trusting Yourself Within the Team

Trust is not only about others.

You must also trust your own role within the group.

In football, insecurity creates hesitation. If you doubt your ability constantly, you avoid involvement. You pass prematurely. You shrink.

Confidence supports connection.

In life, believing you are worthy of belonging allows you to contribute openly.

If you feel you must constantly prove your value, trust feels fragile.

Trust grows when you understand that contribution does not require perfection.

You are part of the system not because you are flawless, but because you are committed.

The Risk That Makes Growth Possible

Trust always carries risk.

The ball might be intercepted. The effort might not be returned. The support might not be equal.

Yet without risk, there is no flow.

In football, teams that refuse risk become predictable. In life, relationships without vulnerability remain shallow.

Trust deepens connection.

It says, I am willing to rely on you. I am willing to support you. I am willing to share both success and failure.

That willingness strengthens more than isolation ever could.

Closing Reflection

You cannot play an entire match alone.

You cannot live a meaningful life alone.

Trust distributes effort, multiplies strength, and sustains momentum.

Yes, it involves uncertainty.

But certainty without connection is emptiness.

Pass the ball.

Share the weight.

Let others move with you.

That is how the game grows larger than one person.

10: Operating as a Team: You Can Only Go So Far Alone

"Individual brilliance wins moments. Collective unity wins seasons."

The Myth of the Solo Performance

There is a strong cultural admiration for individual success.

We celebrate the striker who scores the decisive goal. We replay the highlight that shows one player beating defenders. We tell stories of singular greatness.

Football allows moments of individual brilliance, but it never sustains them alone.

A goal may come from one foot, but it was built through many movements. A defensive stand may hinge on one tackle, but it relies on coordinated positioning.

Life often encourages the illusion that success is solitary.

Work harder. Be independent. Rely on yourself.

Independence has value. But isolation limits growth.

You can achieve something alone.
You cannot sustain everything alone.

Coordination Over Competition

Within a team, roles overlap but do not compete.

If two players chase the same space constantly, structure collapses. If everyone tries to lead every moment, direction becomes unclear.

Effective teams coordinate.

They communicate intention. They recognize strengths. They adjust to each other's movements.

In life, many conflicts arise not from opposition, but from lack of coordination.

Two people want to help, but they move without clarity. Two leaders want progress, but they pull in different directions.

Unity is not sameness.

It is alignment.

Ego and Collective Balance

Ego disrupts teams quietly.

Not always through arrogance, but through subtle self-prioritization. Wanting recognition. Wanting control. Wanting credit.

In football, ego can cause hesitation in passing or reluctance to track back defensively. The player protects personal reputation over collective rhythm.

In life, ego appears in conversations where listening stops. In partnerships where compromise feels like loss.

Balancing ego does not mean diminishing yourself.

It means remembering that contribution matters more than spotlight.

The team grows stronger when individuals are secure enough not to dominate.

Communication as Foundation

Teams that function well communicate constantly.

They adjust positioning. They warn of pressure. They celebrate effort.

Communication prevents misunderstanding from becoming conflict.

In life, silence often creates assumptions. Assumptions create distance.

Clear communication does not eliminate disagreement. It clarifies intention.

Speak honestly.
Listen fully.
Adjust when necessary.

Operating as a team requires dialogue.

Resilience Through Unity

Every season includes setbacks.

Losses. Injuries. Mistakes.

A team built only on individual momentum fractures under pressure. A team built on shared accountability endures.

In life, collective resilience works the same way.

When difficulty arises, those who have built trust and alignment withstand it better. Support circulates. Encouragement balances fatigue.

Unity does not prevent hardship.

It makes hardship survivable.

Knowing When to Step Forward

Operating as a team does not mean constant equality of effort.

Sometimes someone must step forward. Sometimes someone must carry more weight.

In football, a captain may steady the team during chaos. A defender may sacrifice energy to preserve structure.

In life, there are seasons where you lead more. There are seasons where you support more.

Balance over time matters more than perfect balance in every moment.

Teamwork is dynamic.

Letting Others Shine

Healthy teams celebrate individual contribution without resentment.

When someone succeeds, it elevates the group.

Insecurity turns others' success into threat. Confidence turns it into shared achievement.

In life, supporting others does not diminish you.

Recognition is not a limited resource.

The more you uplift others, the stronger the environment becomes.

Closing Reflection

You can move quickly alone.

You can move farther together.

Operating as a team requires humility, communication, patience, and shared responsibility.

It asks you to balance individuality with unity.

The game becomes richer when everyone moves with intention.

Life does too.

11: The Midfield Mindset: Balance and Adaptability

"The middle of the field is where control is quiet and influence is constant."

The Space Between Extremes

In football, the midfield is rarely the most glamorous area of the pitch.

Goals are celebrated at one end. Heroic saves are remembered at the other. The middle often goes unnoticed.

Yet the midfield determines rhythm.

It connects defense to attack. It slows the game when needed. It accelerates when opportunity appears. It absorbs pressure and redistributes it.

The middle is balance.

Life demands a similar mindset.

We often live at extremes. Overworking or disengaging. Reacting emotionally or withdrawing completely. Pushing forward without pause or hesitating without movement.

Balance does not attract attention, but it sustains progress.

Adapting Without Losing Identity

Midfielders adjust constantly.

One moment they are defending. The next they are creating. They shift roles fluidly depending on what the game requires.

Adaptability is their strength.

In life, rigidity creates friction.

Situations change. People evolve. Circumstances shift without warning. If you insist on responding the same way every time, you limit your growth.

Adaptability does not mean abandoning your values. It means applying them wisely in different contexts.

You remain grounded while adjusting.

That combination creates stability.

Emotional Regulation

The midfield is often crowded.

Space is limited. Pressure is frequent. Decisions must be made quickly.

Panic spreads easily in congestion.

Players who thrive in the middle remain calm. They simplify. They choose the clear option instead of the dramatic one.

In life, emotional congestion happens often.

Deadlines. Conflict. Uncertainty. Competing responsibilities.

If you allow emotion to dictate every reaction, you lose clarity.

Calm is not the absence of feeling.

It is the ability to process feeling without being overwhelmed by it.

Regulation creates influence.

Seeing Both Directions

Midfielders must be aware of what is behind them and what lies ahead.

They receive the ball facing pressure, yet they must turn forward when space opens.

This dual awareness requires confidence.

In life, you must hold your past and your future in view without being trapped by either.

Learn from what has already happened. Prepare for what may come. Stay present in what is unfolding.

Balance exists between reflection and anticipation.

Too much of one distorts perception.

Support Without Spotlight

Midfield influence is subtle.

It does not always appear in statistics. It does not always draw applause.

But without it, structure collapses.

In life, many meaningful contributions are quiet.

Stability in a family.
Consistency in a workplace.
Reliability in friendship.

Not everything impactful is visible.

Recognizing the value of subtle influence strengthens self-worth.

You do not need constant validation to matter.

Knowing When to Advance

Balance does not mean neutrality.

Midfielders must recognize moments to push forward. To break lines. To create opportunity.

Playing safe forever limits potential.

In life, balance includes courage.

You assess risk carefully. You move intentionally. You step forward when alignment is clear.

Adaptability includes boldness.

Staying centered does not require staying passive.

Preventing Burnout

Because the midfield connects everything, it risks exhaustion.

Covering space constantly drains energy. Without awareness, fatigue accumulates.

Life operates similarly.

If you are the connector in every environment, you must protect your energy. You cannot solve every problem or mediate every conflict.

Balance includes boundaries.

Rest is not indulgence. It is maintenance.

Without recovery, influence weakens.

Closing Reflection

The middle of the field is rarely celebrated, yet it shapes everything.

Balance allows adaptation. Adaptation sustains progress.

Life is rarely lived at the edges alone.

It unfolds in the middle, where restraint meets movement, where stability meets change.

Develop the midfield mindset.

Stay centered.
Adjust wisely.
Move with intention.

And let quiet influence guide the game.

12: Visualization: Seeing the Play Before It Happens

"The clearest moves are often made long before the moment arrives."

Preparing the Mind Before the Moment

In football, the body reacts quickly.

But the mind moves first.

Before receiving the ball, experienced players have already imagined what might happen. They have rehearsed movements in training. They have pictured angles and spaces repeatedly.

When the moment comes, it feels familiar.

Visualization does not guarantee success. It reduces shock.

Life benefits from the same preparation.

Difficult conversations. Important decisions. High-pressure situations. These moments feel overwhelming when they arrive without mental rehearsal.

When you take time to imagine how you want to respond, you increase steadiness.

You are not guessing in the moment. You are executing something considered.

Clarity Through Rehearsal

Visualization is not fantasy.

It is disciplined rehearsal.

In football, players visualize controlling the ball cleanly. They imagine composure under pressure. They picture success not to inflate confidence, but to reinforce readiness.

In life, mental rehearsal clarifies intention.

How will I respond if I feel criticized?
How will I maintain calm if tension rises?
What words align with my values?

When the situation arrives, your reaction is less chaotic.

The mind recognizes the path.

Reducing Fear of the Unknown

Fear often grows from uncertainty.

When you have never imagined an outcome, your mind fills the gap with worst-case scenarios.

Visualization reduces that uncertainty.

It introduces familiarity.

In football, players rehearse penalty kicks not because they expect every match to end in one, but because preparation reduces anxiety.

In life, imagining success and resilience does not eliminate risk. It reduces paralysis.

You begin to believe that you can navigate what arrives.

Belief strengthens response.

Seeing Beyond Immediate Pressure

Visualization is not limited to specific actions.

It includes seeing the broader picture.

In football, players anticipate how one pass can create space three movements later. They visualize sequences, not isolated touches.

Life requires similar perspective.

A single choice rarely stands alone. It influences relationships, habits, long-term direction.

Seeing beyond the immediate moment reduces impulsiveness.

You act with awareness of consequence.

Aligning Action With Identity

Visualization works best when grounded in identity.

It is not about imagining perfection. It is about imagining integrity.

In football, a defender visualizes staying disciplined. A midfielder imagines calm distribution. They do not imagine being someone else. They reinforce who they are.

In life, clarity increases when you ask:

What kind of person do I want to be in this situation?
What response aligns with my values?

Visualization strengthens alignment.

When action matches identity, confidence grows naturally.

Avoiding Overcontrol

There is a difference between preparation and control.

Visualization prepares you. It does not script reality.

In football, no amount of rehearsal prevents every unexpected bounce or unpredictable movement.

In life, circumstances shift beyond your planning.

The purpose of visualization is flexibility, not rigidity.

You prepare to respond wisely, not to control every outcome.

That distinction protects adaptability.

Reinforcing Confidence Through Memory

Visualization also involves remembering.

Recall past moments when you handled pressure well. Remember times when patience served you. Reflect on instances where restraint prevented regret.

Confidence is strengthened by evidence.

In football, reviewing successful plays builds belief. In life, acknowledging growth reinforces resilience.

You have navigated difficulty before.

Remembering that changes how you approach what comes next.

Closing Reflection

The clearest movements are rarely spontaneous.

They are supported by preparation.

See the play before it unfolds.
Rehearse calm before tension arrives.
Imagine integrity before challenge tests you.

Visualization does not remove uncertainty.

It steadies you within it.

And when the moment finally comes, your response feels less like reaction and more like intention.

13: Fitness and Form: Discipline and Growth

"Form comes and goes. What you build underneath stays."

The Difference Between Feeling Good and Being Ready

There are days in football when everything clicks.

Your legs feel light. Decisions come easily. The game flows. You anticipate space effortlessly. Passes connect. Movement feels natural.

That is form.

Then there are days when none of that is true.

Your touch is slightly off. Timing feels delayed. You work harder for smaller results. Confidence feels fragile.

Fitness is different.

Fitness does not depend on feeling good. It carries you when you do not.

Life reveals the same contrast.

Motivation rises and falls. Confidence fluctuates. Energy shifts with circumstance.

Discipline is what remains when inspiration fades.

Building Beneath the Surface

Fitness is not built during matches. It is built quietly.

Training sessions. Repetition. Recovery. Attention to detail.

Much of this work is invisible.

Life growth works the same way.

Habits formed in private shape performance in public. Small routines, consistent effort, steady reflection. These foundations rarely attract attention, but they sustain you when pressure increases.

What you build underneath determines how you stand when form weakens.

Consistency Over Intensity

Intense effort feels powerful.

It creates momentum. It produces visible results quickly.

But intensity without consistency fades.

In football, a player who trains sporadically cannot rely on form alone. When pressure increases, inconsistency shows.

In life, bursts of productivity cannot replace steady discipline.

Reading occasionally does not build understanding. Exercising briefly does not build endurance. Communicating only during crisis does not build trust.

Consistency compounds quietly.

Small, repeated actions accumulate into strength.

Accepting Cycles

Form is cyclical.

No player maintains peak performance indefinitely. Confidence dips. External factors intervene. Fatigue appears.

Expecting constant excellence creates unnecessary frustration.

In life, growth also follows cycles.

Periods of clarity are followed by uncertainty. Seasons of progress are followed by stagnation.

Understanding this rhythm prevents overreaction.

A difficult week does not erase years of effort. A slow period does not define your capacity.

Fitness carries you through the cycle.

Discipline Without Harshness

Discipline is often misunderstood as rigidity.

In football, discipline includes rest. Recovery. Listening to the body.

Ignoring fatigue leads to injury.

In life, discipline requires balance.

You hold yourself accountable, but you do not punish yourself endlessly. You pursue growth, but you allow recovery.

Harshness drains motivation.

Sustainable discipline respects limits.

Returning to Fundamentals

When form declines, experienced players return to basics.

Simple passes. Controlled touches. Clear positioning.

They do not attempt brilliance while unstable.

In life, when clarity fades, fundamentals restore balance.

Sleep properly.
Eat consistently.
Speak honestly.
Simplify commitments.

Growth does not always require dramatic change.

Sometimes it requires steady return.

Measuring Progress Quietly

Fitness improvement is gradual.

Small increases in stamina. Slight improvements in strength. Subtle gains in balance.

Progress often feels invisible until a demanding moment reveals it.

In life, development unfolds similarly.

Patience grows without announcement. Emotional regulation strengthens quietly. Perspective deepens over time.

You may not notice change daily.

But pressure reveals preparation.

Closing Reflection

Form will rise and fall.

Motivation will fluctuate.

Confidence will shift.

What remains is what you build consistently.

Discipline is not loud. It does not demand attention.

It works in the background, shaping resilience.

When form fades, fitness carries you.

When inspiration weakens, habit steadies you.

Build beneath the surface.

That foundation will outlast every temporary peak.

14: The Manager Within: Coaching Yourself

"The voice you listen to most will shape the game you play."

The Inner Voice

Every team has a manager.

Someone who observes from a wider perspective. Someone who adjusts strategy. Someone who decides when to push and when to protect.

But players also carry another presence with them onto the field.

An internal voice.

It comments on mistakes. It celebrates good moments. It questions decisions. It evaluates effort.

In life, that internal voice is constant.

Sometimes it motivates. Sometimes it criticizes. Sometimes it doubts.

The way you manage that voice determines much of your experience.

Self-Talk Under Pressure

In football, pressure exposes the quality of inner dialogue.

After a missed chance, one player may think, I am useless. Another may think, focus on the next touch.

The external situation is identical. The internal response shapes the outcome.

Life follows this pattern closely.

When something goes wrong, your inner voice speaks first.

It can say, this always happens to me.
Or it can say, adjust and continue.

Self-talk influences behavior more than circumstance.

Coaching Without Cruelty

Some players believe harsh self-criticism drives improvement.

They scold themselves relentlessly. They replay mistakes obsessively.

Short term, this may create urgency. Long term, it erodes confidence.

Effective managers correct without humiliating.

They identify error clearly. They adjust tactics. They maintain belief.

In life, self-coaching requires the same balance.

Honesty without cruelty.
Accountability without self-destruction.

You can acknowledge a mistake without defining yourself by it.

Setting Standards

A manager sets standards.

Effort levels. Discipline. Commitment.

Without standards, performance drifts.

In life, self-leadership involves defining your own expectations.

What behavior aligns with who you want to be?
What habits support your long-term direction?
What boundaries protect your energy?

Standards create structure.

But structure must be realistic.

Unreasonable expectations create constant disappointment. Measured standards create growth.

Adjusting Strategy

Not every approach works forever.

In football, managers adapt to opponents. They change formations. They substitute players when necessary.

In life, self-coaching includes flexibility.

If a routine no longer serves you, adjust it. If a goal has changed meaning, reassess it. If an environment consistently drains you, consider new positioning.

Rigid persistence is not always strength.

Adaptation reflects awareness.

Taking Responsibility

The manager cannot play the match. The players execute.

Similarly, your inner voice can guide, but action is yours.

Blaming circumstances endlessly removes agency.

In football, complaining about conditions does not alter the score. In life, focusing only on external obstacles reduces initiative.

Self-coaching involves asking difficult questions.

What can I control?
What must I accept?
Where do I need to improve?

Responsibility strengthens clarity.

Encouragement as Fuel

A good manager recognizes effort.

They acknowledge improvement. They reinforce progress.

Encouragement is not flattery. It is reinforcement of growth.

In life, recognizing your own effort sustains motivation.

Celebrate discipline.
Acknowledge resilience.
Notice small victories.

Constant criticism drains energy. Balanced encouragement restores it.

Knowing When to Rest

Managers protect players from burnout.

They rotate squads. They schedule recovery.

In life, pushing relentlessly without pause creates diminishing returns.

Rest is not weakness. It is strategic.

Self-coaching includes permission to recover.

Without recovery, even the strongest performance declines.

Closing Reflection

The voice inside you shapes your experience more than external commentary.

Coach yourself wisely.

Correct without cruelty.
Set standards with compassion.
Adapt when necessary.
Encourage consistently.

You are both player and manager in your own life.

Lead yourself with clarity.

And the game becomes steadier.

15: Injury Time: Recovery and Resilience

"Not every pause is the end. Some are invitations to rebuild."

When the Game Stops

In football, injury changes everything.

The rhythm breaks. The pace slows. What felt stable suddenly becomes uncertain.

A player who was central to movement is now watching from the sidelines. The body that once responded instantly now demands patience.

Injury feels like interruption.

Life introduces its own versions.

Unexpected loss.
Burnout.
Failure.
Illness.
Emotional exhaustion.

These moments stop forward motion.

They challenge identity.

The Loss of Momentum

Momentum feels powerful.

When it is taken away, frustration follows.

In football, an injured player struggles not only with physical pain but with displacement. Teammates continue playing. The season advances. Time moves forward.

In life, when progress stalls, comparison intensifies. Others appear to move ahead while you are recovering.

Resilience begins by accepting that interruption is part of the cycle.

You cannot rush healing without consequence.

Reframing the Pause

Injury time is not only about absence.

It is about recalibration.

During recovery, players observe differently. They study the game from new angles. They strengthen neglected areas. They rebuild fundamentals.

Life's pauses offer similar opportunities.

Reflection deepens. Perspective sharpens. Values clarify.

When forced to slow down, you notice patterns that speed once concealed.

Pain often carries information.

The Patience of Healing

Recovery requires patience that ambition resists.

In football, returning too early risks reinjury. Pushing the body before it is ready prolongs absence.

In life, emotional wounds follow similar principles.

Forcing closure before processing pain creates unresolved tension. Pretending strength before stability leads to collapse.

Healing demands honesty.

Admitting weakness does not erase strength. It protects it.

Redefining Strength

Strength is often associated with endurance.

Pushing through discomfort. Ignoring fatigue. Continuing despite warning signs.

But resilience is not constant exertion.

In football, disciplined recovery prevents long-term damage. In life, sustainable growth includes rest and recalibration.

Strength includes vulnerability.

It allows you to acknowledge limitation without surrendering identity.

Learning from Setback

Injury changes perspective.

A player who once took movement for granted now appreciates basic participation. Gratitude grows where frustration once lived.

Life setbacks reshape priorities.

You recognize what truly matters. Relationships regain significance. Small victories feel meaningful.

Resilience is not denial of difficulty. It is transformation through it.

Returning to the Field

Coming back from injury carries uncertainty.

Confidence must rebuild. Timing must recalibrate. Trust in the body must return.

Progress is gradual.

In life, returning after hardship follows similar steps.

You test boundaries carefully. You rebuild routines. You regain rhythm slowly.

Patience during return protects progress.

You are not the same person you were before interruption.

You are more aware.

Closing Reflection

Injury time feels inconvenient.

It disrupts plans. It challenges identity. It exposes vulnerability.

But within pause lies potential.

Recovery rebuilds strength differently. Resilience grows from reflection. Perspective deepens through interruption.

Not every halt is failure.

Some are preparation.

When you return to movement, you carry more than before.

You carry understanding.

And that changes how you play the rest of the game.

16: Suffering: Embracing Life's Challenges

"Pain is not the opposite of growth. It is often the path toward it."

The Reality of Hard Matches

Not every match is beautiful.

Some are messy. Physical. Frustrating. Nothing flows easily. Every movement requires effort.

In those matches, skill alone is not enough.

You rely on endurance. On discipline. On composure.

Life presents similar stretches.

There are seasons when nothing feels effortless. Plans collapse. Effort goes unnoticed. Progress seems distant.

Suffering does not announce itself politely.

It interrupts comfort.

Why We Resist Discomfort

Discomfort feels unnatural.

We are taught to avoid it, minimize it, escape it.

In football, players instinctively avoid physical strain. They conserve energy. They protect themselves.

But growth often lives within resistance.

Endurance strengthens through strain. Skill sharpens through challenge.

In life, discomfort signals friction between who you are and who you are becoming.

Avoiding all difficulty prevents development.

Embracing challenge builds capacity.

Distinguishing Pain from Harm

Not all pain is productive.

In football, pain from effort differs from injury. One strengthens. The other damages.

In life, emotional discomfort from growth differs from harm.

Constructive pain teaches. It stretches perspective. It deepens empathy.

Destructive harm requires protection and boundaries.

Wisdom lies in recognizing the difference.

Growth asks for endurance.
Self-respect demands protection.

Finding Meaning Within Struggle

Matches that test endurance often reveal character.

When fatigue sets in, discipline matters. When confidence wavers, composure matters.

Life's challenges expose similar truths.

Difficult conversations reveal patience. Loss reveals resilience. Failure reveals humility.

Suffering does not automatically create growth.

Reflection does.

Without reflection, pain becomes bitterness.

With reflection, pain becomes understanding.

Shared Struggle

No team survives hardship alone.

Players encourage one another. They communicate more deliberately. They tighten structure.

In life, isolation amplifies suffering.

Sharing difficulty does not eliminate it, but it distributes weight.

Honest conversation reduces loneliness. Support strengthens endurance.

Struggle becomes lighter when it is not hidden.

The Long View

A difficult match is one chapter in a season.

When viewed in isolation, it feels overwhelming. When placed within context, it becomes part of a larger narrative.

Life challenges often feel permanent while they are unfolding.

Stepping back provides perspective.

This moment is part of a longer story. It is shaping qualities you may not recognize immediately.

Endurance rarely feels meaningful in the moment.

Its value appears later.

Strength Refined Through Fire

Pressure refines.

In football, high-stakes matches reveal preparation. Weakness becomes visible. Strength becomes undeniable.

In life, hardship clarifies priorities.

What once seemed urgent may lose importance. What once seemed trivial may gain depth.

Suffering refines attention.

It strips away illusion.

Closing Reflection

Suffering is not a detour from life.

It is woven into it.

You cannot eliminate all difficulty. You can influence how you engage with it.

Endure when growth is forming.
Protect yourself when harm appears.
Reflect so that pain transforms into wisdom.

The hardest matches often teach the most enduring lessons.

And when you emerge from them, you carry strength that comfort alone could never build.

17: Full-Time: Legacy and Extra Time

"The final whistle does not measure how loud you were. It measures how well you played your part."

When the Whistle Blows

Every match ends.

The whistle sounds. Movement stops. The scoreboard settles into permanence.

For ninety minutes, everything felt urgent. Decisions carried weight. Effort demanded focus.

Then suddenly, it is over.

Life contains similar moments.

Projects conclude. Roles shift. Seasons close. Relationships change form. Phases of identity transition quietly.

We do not always hear a clear whistle.

But endings arrive.

What Remains After Applause Fades

After full-time, statistics remain. But what lingers more deeply are impressions.

Did the team move with cohesion?
Did effort reflect commitment?
Did players honor their roles?

In life, reputation is shaped less by isolated achievements and more by consistent character.

How you treated others.
How you handled difficulty.
How you responded to failure.

Legacy is rarely dramatic.

It is cumulative.

The Quiet Measure of Contribution

Scorelines attract attention.

Contribution often hides beneath them.

In football, a player may never score yet transform the rhythm of a match. Their positioning prevents danger. Their composure stabilizes movement.

In life, impact works the same way.

Influence may not be visible. Kindness may not trend. Stability may not be celebrated.

Yet these quiet contributions shape environments.

Legacy grows from consistency.

Extra Time

Sometimes matches extend beyond expectation.

Extra time tests endurance. Fatigue deepens. Small decisions carry amplified consequence.

In life, extra time appears in unexpected ways.

Second chances.
Late opportunities.
Renewed purpose after loss.

These moments feel different.

You are more aware. More reflective. More deliberate.

Extra time invites intention.

You recognize that energy is finite. You choose more carefully how to spend it.

Acceptance Without Regret

Full-time brings evaluation.

Regret may surface. Opportunities missed. Mistakes remembered.

But dwelling endlessly on what cannot be changed distorts closure.

In football, players review performance to improve, not to punish themselves.

In life, reflection should guide growth, not anchor shame.

Accept imperfection.

Growth is measured over seasons, not isolated moments.

Playing Until the End

Some players disengage when the outcome seems decided.

Others continue with discipline, regardless of score.

Integrity is revealed when attention fades.

In life, effort when unseen defines character.

How you act when no one is watching shapes your internal narrative.

Consistency builds self-respect.

What Truly Matters

At full-time, trophies matter less than connection.

Shared struggle. Collective effort. Lessons learned.

In life, relationships endure longer than achievements.

Titles fade. Applause quiets. Recognition shifts.

What remains are moments of integrity, courage, patience, and compassion.

These shape memory.

Closing Reflection

The final whistle does not ask how impressive you appeared.

It asks how faithfully you participated.

Did you show up honestly?
Did you honor your role?
Did you move with intention?

Life, like football, ends eventually.

The goal is not perfection.

It is presence.

Play fully.
Adjust when needed.
Trust others.
Grow through difficulty.

When full-time arrives, let it find you steady.

Not because the game was flawless.

But because you played it well.

About the Author

Vaibhav Joshi explores football not merely as a sport, but as a framework for understanding life.

His writing reflects on discipline, awareness, resilience, timing, and human connection through the structure and rhythm of the game. Rather than offering formulas or loud conclusions, he examines the internal patterns that shape character under pressure.

Football entered his life long before writing did. It was not always triumphant. It involved doubt, comparison, misplaced effort, and long periods of quiet recalibration. Over time, the game remained about winning, but it also became about understanding what winning truly requires, and how repetition shapes both results and character.

His journey in football began early. At the age of twenty-one, Vaibhav started working as a team manager with the Indian Football Association. What began as a young role close to the dressing room gradually evolved into deeper involvement within the broader Indian football ecosystem. Experiencing the game both as a player and in administrative roles gave him a rare perspective on how football functions beyond the pitch.

Alongside this journey in football, he stepped into the corporate world, working with private equity clients and navigating the pace and expectations of professional life. Moving between the discipline of sport and the demands of corporate environments offered its own education. Both worlds revealed similar truths about responsibility, teamwork, leadership, and the quiet resilience required to grow.

Many of the reflections in this book were not researched. They were lived.

At the core of his work is a belief in genuine connection and in serving others through presence, integrity, love, and gratitude practiced daily rather than spoken occasionally. To him, love is responsibility. Gratitude is awareness.

He continues to see himself as a student of both the game and life, aware that growth is rarely dramatic and almost always deliberate.

If you recognize parts of yourself in these pages, it is because you have already been playing your own match.

9 789357 593267

Printed at Repro India Ltd.